"TIPS TO SUCCESSFULLY PROMOTE AN AFFILIATE PROGRAM"

(Includes 2 great companies to start earning income with)

Written By: Char

Thanks for taking the time to read this eBook. This book is about a great work at home opportunity that you can work anytime and you can also get paid daily. This book will provide you in dept information about a company that can pay you today and explain its mission statement. I will explain to you this great work at home opportunity along with some marketing tips that you can use that is free. I will provide you with some screenshots, templates, and links that you can used to help promote your system. This eBook is base from my real life experience working with this program and many other programs using the same technique. It will answer all your questions. Not many people provide you the resources it takes for you to succeed in this business. I do not hold any information back and if any update is being added to this book you will be notify.

If you've ever been interesting working at home I would recommend affiliating marketing. The reason why I recommend affiliating is because you can earn income the same day and usually get paid the same day. It is also easier to determine if the program is legit. There are a lot of companies similar to ZNZ and I will introduce you to some more programs later own. Right now, we want to stick to something you can get paid daily via PayPal or alert pay. Some affiliate programs requires for you to purchase a product or used the product for a limit time which is a free trial. I really don't mind paying for a product because when I pay for a product I make sure it's something I'm going to need or signup for something just to continue to make profits. For example, a site that I used as well I join the book club because I read a lot and I receive 5 books for 0.25 and plus shipping, but this opportunity makes me $480.00 a payday which is not a lost. That's how you should be looking at ZNZ. ZNZ doesn't have many offers that you can use for yourself, but there are free offers that can come in handy.

Most people get affiliate marketing confuses with MLM also known as pyramid scheme, such as 5linx, Amway and more. I didn't realize that my sponsor was trying to get me involve into Amway until the end of a seminar. One thing that they don't tell you is that you have to have a huge down line in order for you to get to the next level. Plus there are huge fees for you to get started. A lot of your sponsors won't tell you how to get promoted to the next level. Most of them don't even know what they are selling. I also never did understand their commission system which is always a bad sign. Also their products are always something that seems outdated compare to under big brand companies. Usually whenever you search for MLM companies online and do a review you usually see a lot of bad reviews compare to an affiliate company.

This was just a brief introduction about an MLM which is something you won't be doing. You won't need a huge down line. All you need to do is follow these marketing tips and me patient you will start to see profits.

Do you want to make extra income? Is work at home jobs real? Are you tired of looking for a work at home position? Are tired of getting scam? I'm going to introduce to you a company that is great and 100% legit and pay me to sit down and work at home. I'm not going to tell you to quit your day job yet until you get streams of income coming in. I'm going to tell you the company's mission, pros and cons, the pay structure.

Company's Mission

The company is of course a website that they have companies like Direct Tv, Discover, free credit report, and more, which they pay them to advertise their trial offers. Your roll is to referral people and they must complete one of the offers. Technically you are an affiliate, marketer, salesperson, or whichever one you want to be call.

Why it isn't a scam?

There are a couple reasons why this isn't a scam. The obvious reason is because there are Fortune 500 companies like Directv involve and even credit report. The other reason is that the company asks for your tax information whenever you earn a certain amount around $600. Also you can choose to get paid through Paypal, Alertpay, or receive a check (checks you will need more referrals.)

Requirements

The requirement is simple. You must have internet access at home, meaning you cannot use a public computer. The reason why you can used a public computer is to create fake users and have the same person for each profile. (Fraudulent) You must be a citizen of the US, UK, or CA. In order to start referring people you must complete an offer before you get started, which require a credit card. (Use a prepaid card)

Pros

There are a lot of pros I like about the system. The main pros is that I like is that it is free. Now some of the trial offers you have to pay, but the key thing is to always go for the free ones and signup with a prepaid card so you won't be charge. Also they pay daily, meaning you get paid the same day or the next day depend with time of the day you earn income only if you have PayPal or Alertpay. You also can work anytime you want. You also receive bonus. There is also a free marketing system set in place where you can used their auto responder for emails or keep up with stats.

Cons

I don't have too much cons to say. Some folks may not want to submit their credit card information. They also may be concern if their card may get charge, which is why I recommend a prepaid card. Remember when you apply for an offer you will go directly to that company's site, which is secure. Also for the UK and CA there seems to be a lack of free offers.

Pay Structure

I know you have been waiting for this part forever the main part. The company pays $20 per referral which is only one referral. Don't sweat it because if you know 5 people that is an easy $100.00. Now also you can pick your reward. You can get an Ipad 2, IPod Touch, money, or check. They also give you bonus money. There is also a more advance program where you get paid $60 per referral, but you have to complete more than one offer. My advice is for you to promote the $20 one and start working yourself up because you want to figure out which promotion method works for you.

Marketing

The key thing to make money with taking trials is to market ZNZ. You can make even $600.00 a day if you figure out a technique that works for you. It takes a lot of time to actually get traffic to your blog.

Friend and Family- If you really want some fast cash I would recommend this method. As long as you are not in the same house hold if you have at least 10 friends and family that you know will love the opportunity that is $200.00. Plus you can make an extra $480.00 with these contacts.

Email Marketing- I know you are worried about spamming, but if you go on the ftc.gov website or Google it. There is something that is call CANSPAM which is the leak in the system. All it says that if you provide the subscriber a way to opt out of emails, provide your address(PO BOX for your own safety), state that this email is advertisement purpose, and provide your companies information (website) For CA or the UK please review your government's policy on spam.

Also you can send bulk email if you purchase a software, but you still have to used some type of SMTP server. (For ex Google, Hotmail) For Google you can send 500 emails per day the most. I usually switch over when I hit the limit (the software will let you know. I highly recommend you purchase this software because its fast and it goes directly to the person's inbox and not spam.

I wouldn't recommend Aweber for beginners because you will have to have a subscribers list already, but there is a free trial available for $1.

I would recommend you to put a subject , but please don't put something like Work at Home, because of the simple fact there are a lot of work at home scams and it may run the reader away. You want to make it like a company that is hiring for a real position For ex: Sales, Customer Service

Lead Scraping Software- I actually owned great lead scraping software that I can put a domain name and it will return a whole bunch of emails. I won't recommend you to purchase buy this tool, because you will have to email millions of leads per day, which of course it is impossible to email millions of leads per day.

Buying Leads- Buying Leads is the last thing I would recommend. To get quality leads you have to pay like $500 for at least 200 leads especially for free programs. All leads are is people that had fill out information looking for more information on business opportunity. I would recommend this method for MLM

Press Release- There are 100's of free press release sites, but before you start a press release please be AWARE that a lot of press release don't like affiliate links regardless if you have a website they will find out and deny you. I know this one press release that you can get approve right away so if you want the information to that press release please inbox me. It's all about saving time and helping others.

Post Cards- I would recommend GotPrint because they have one of the best prices. I recommend you get at least 100 for a trial and error test. I would also recommend you manually dig up leads, like dig up resumes online. Whatever you do please don't buy any leads. Some lead companies you may have a conversion rate, but it's for a steep price. post cards it's not the most effective method because you have to order like 100s of them

I also recommend you to use their template because I spend all day just to get the proper size. (the bleed size they call it). I'm going to show you a simple of a postcard that I did that you can used the exact same format for one of my sites, but. That was my rough draft.

Results: I would never recommend this method because it's a small ratio that you will get any results. Unless, you do 5,000 cards and you may make at least $300.00. I only did 100 cards and I haven't got any results.

Banner Ads- Banner Ads can be expensive, but there are free ways you can get a banner exchange which you post someone else's banner on your site and you do the same in return for traffic. There are a lot of sites that you can purchase banner ads for a low price, but before you make any purchase make sure the site is rank high on the Alexa usually 100,000 and under.

Dollar Bills- I know it may sound strange to you, but if you put your website name on a dollar bill it will get around in so many hands. Who asks for change for a $1?

Flyers- Start passing those flyers out on school campus, train stops, bus stations, Department of labor. Even your local gas station! Even church! Someone always complain at church, "I wish I get bless with a job! You give them a flyer and you get bless with money!

Business Cards- You can purchase business cards at a very reasonable price. I would recommend the same strategy for flyers. You can also get it at Got Print or just get you some business card templates from Wal-Mart and really save!

Newspaper Ads- Newspaper ads can be pretty tricky because you have to do your research to see how many people buy the magazine. Also posting in the business opportunity can be very risky because there are a lot of tacky ads posting as a work at home opportunity and their really not legit. I would risk posting in the employment area under the sales or customer service area. It all depends what your budget is, but newspaper ads can become expensive.

Magazine Ads- Magazine ads is something I highly recommend. It is very expensive especially if you want to get a whole page. There are a lot of works at home or small business magazines that you can target. I wouldn't recommend classifying at the back of the magazine because it looks s clutter and you want your ad to stand out more.

Ezine Articles- One of the most common ways to get traffic to your URL. It is like a 5 day approval process, but you can speed the time up if you submit at least five more articles. Ezine Articles is very particular because you have to write in proper grammar and you have to have a certain amount of words. There are a lot of alternative such as Goarticles.

Social Network- This is the most popular method which is at no cost. Facebook is the most popular because of the amount of traffic. It's always good to add people that are internet marketers because they can give you free advice. Joining groups and posting comments that is pertaining to the subject and no spamming is a good way to meet clients although it can take a lot of time. Especially for Facebook I wouldn't be concern with how much likes you have because people can still view your page.

Classified Ads- One of the classified ads I recommend for trials and money is Craigslist. I just look under people that are looking for jobs and I call them. This method can take awhile because not too many people are comfortable with it. I don't post ads because it is $25 if you live in a major city. Some free classified ads such as back page is pretty hard to list ads because they mark everything as scam so it's best to contact people in their forums. I recently had an experience with Craigslist and I notice that when you post ads in the small business area you don't get any replies. The most likely reason is because people are posting all kinds of programs that are cheesy and may not be legit. I would recommend you posting at the work at home classified ads.

      Sites that accept HTML like Craigslist I recommend you to do a click on image because it makes it stand out more. You can use Photobucket to get the HTML code for your image. I won't spend too much time posting classified ads because it has a low conversion rate. You

Freelancers- Freelancers is usually the last method I used because sometimes the fees can be pretty expensive and when it comes to getting referrals it seems that they pretty much lack at. The time it takes to explain what you are looking for can be time consuming.

Gigbucks- This is one of my favorite websites because every gig I purchase which is usually $5 and they perform their job very well. There are allot of similar sites (Fiverr,Taskarmy, etc) and for that price you can easily make the money right back. (WARNING: Please Stay Away From the Software)

Search engines- This is one of my favorite methods that I've manage to master. I've recently have one of my website rank on the first page of Google and I had my week of fame, but unfortunately it is number 6. I feel kind of relief because I have a YouTube video that is on type and I highly recommend to used it as a backup in case your URL fails into ranking. In my next eBook I'll explain how to methods I used to get rank high on Google, which includes getting onto the first page, troubleshooting steps to take if you're not ranking high, and also sites that can help you get back links for free.

FCM- This is known as the free cash machine where it displays all your stats and emails. I don't think it is too accurate, but it is 100% free and it will give you resources to other marketing tools. There are a lot of tools you can used such as auto responses templates which I don't used. You can also keep up with your leads and stats. You can also attend the daily webinar.

Forums- This is the most effective methods to getting referrals. In order to get sign ups you must keep posting on the forum along with your website after the end of each post. Notice I didn't said affiliate links because the admin may get offend and disapprove your post and plus it looks tacky. You want to post on forums like work at home forums not a golfing forum.

Website- This is my favorite subject to talk about because this is one of my main sources to get traffic and advertise how I want. You can set up your auto responder system, video market system, or whatever you want to market. I like to set up my website with Wordpress which is a free tool with wonderful plug-ins that you can keep track of traffic. It's always good to keep it short and sample. I recommend a .com, .net, org,.co because it seems to rank well with Google. I never had any success with .info because search engines consider it spammed and it's hard to get rank with a.info. More than likely you won't find an .info domain name ranking on the front the page. My next eBook I will go more into SEO and technique that it takes to rank on the front page. Wordpress has a plug-in that you can set up an auto responder which is free and can install in within minutes.

Wordpress Audio Responder Plug-in- Go to Install Plug-in and type in WP Auto Responder

Squidoo, Hubpages- These are one of my two favorite sites because it's free to promote and you can get a lot of views. To create a Squidoo lens it usually takes 30 minutes because you have to complete a certain percentage of your lens to get approve. Hubpages it is a lot faster, but make sure you don't used your affiliate link because your article will get banned.

Google Keywords-I have used Google Keywords in the past whenever I had received a $75 free coupon which is not a lot. You can apply these principles to any keyword system. You should choose your words by using the Google keyword tools and of course check the lowest search word result, usually 2,000 local results and I assume that I will receive at least 850 hits and at least 30 sales. Always use Google Keyword Tool as your guide when selecting your keywords.

Google Analytics- This is a must used tool to have. It gives you an update on how much traffic you receive. It is free.

SEO- You're probably tired of me talking about SEO, but SEO is 100% free. Whatever contact you write always makes sure it is revolve around using great keywords that help you get good ranking. I don't worry about how much back links you get because you will need like 100 thousand back links.

Leverage

This is one of the keywords you should be familiar with in any business or in any situation. One of the reasons I like affiliating is because you can used the goods you purchase and also get paid for referring others. ZNZ you can make $20-$60 per person. You can also referral your leads to a new opportunity which is similar call 360elite, but you have to purchase an item. Of course I didn't mine because I brought 5 books and paid $12. You should never have idle leads hanging around. Always may sure you keep contacting them.

Summary

I give you all the marketing techniques that I used and I'm going to give you a summary and some tricks that I use. You should utilize all the free methods before you pay for anything. To get started I would recommend you getting your own website which you can start for a little as $8.00 for a .com domain name. There are a lot of places you can purchase a domain name. I used 1and1 and then I switch over to 000webhost, which I've updated my packet for unlimited hosting. Next I install Wordpress and that is pretty much it. I write a lot of articles because it helps drives traffic. One thing you have to remember when dealing with anything online is whatever article you write you always want to make sure you write contact that is base around keywords especially in your domain name and the first couple of sentence. The key thing is to always revolve using the SEO basics which is for free traffic. The next couple of pages will be templates and screenshots of this opportunity also a link that you can sign up at.

This is a screenshot of the different prizes you can get. You can get paid daily through paypal and alert pay which is one referral. Checks is 2 Referrals. The Iphone 4 you need 27 referrals, Ipad 216GB you need 21 Referrals. The Custom order is when you can pick your own prize. To learn more visit **http://tinyurl.com/5ssyqwn**

This is some of the offers that you have to complete one to start making monkey. It's a total of 35 which the number changes. Some of them are free. **http://tinyurl.com/5ssyqwn**

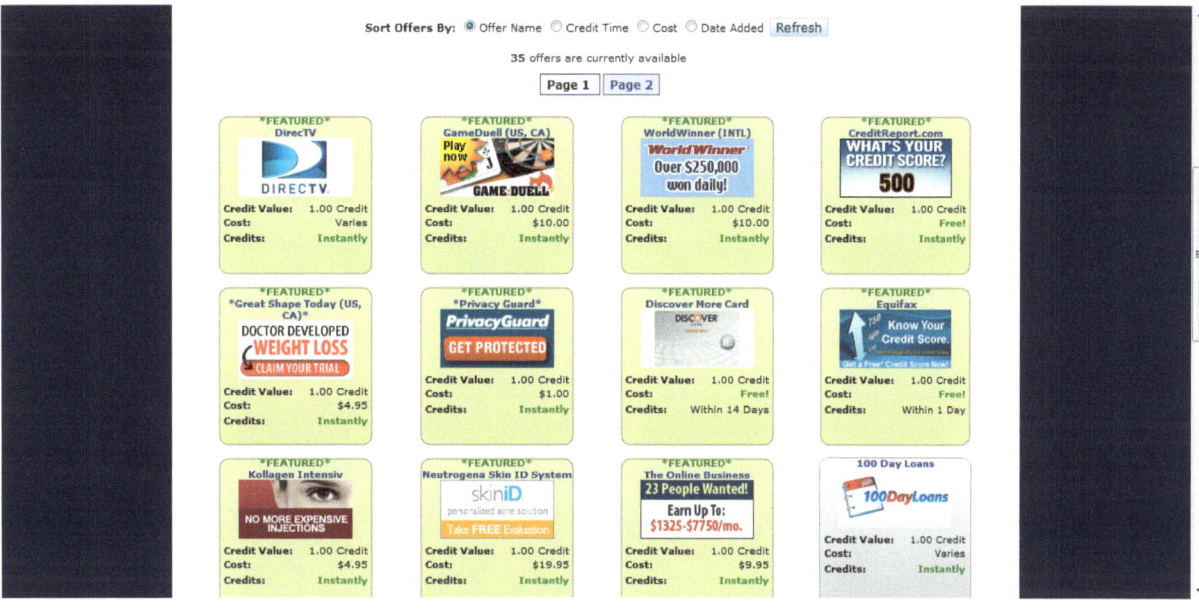

This is the free cash machine back office. I don't used it anymore. It give you resources like autoresponder, banner ads, and more. **https://fcmtraining.com/members/fcm-login**

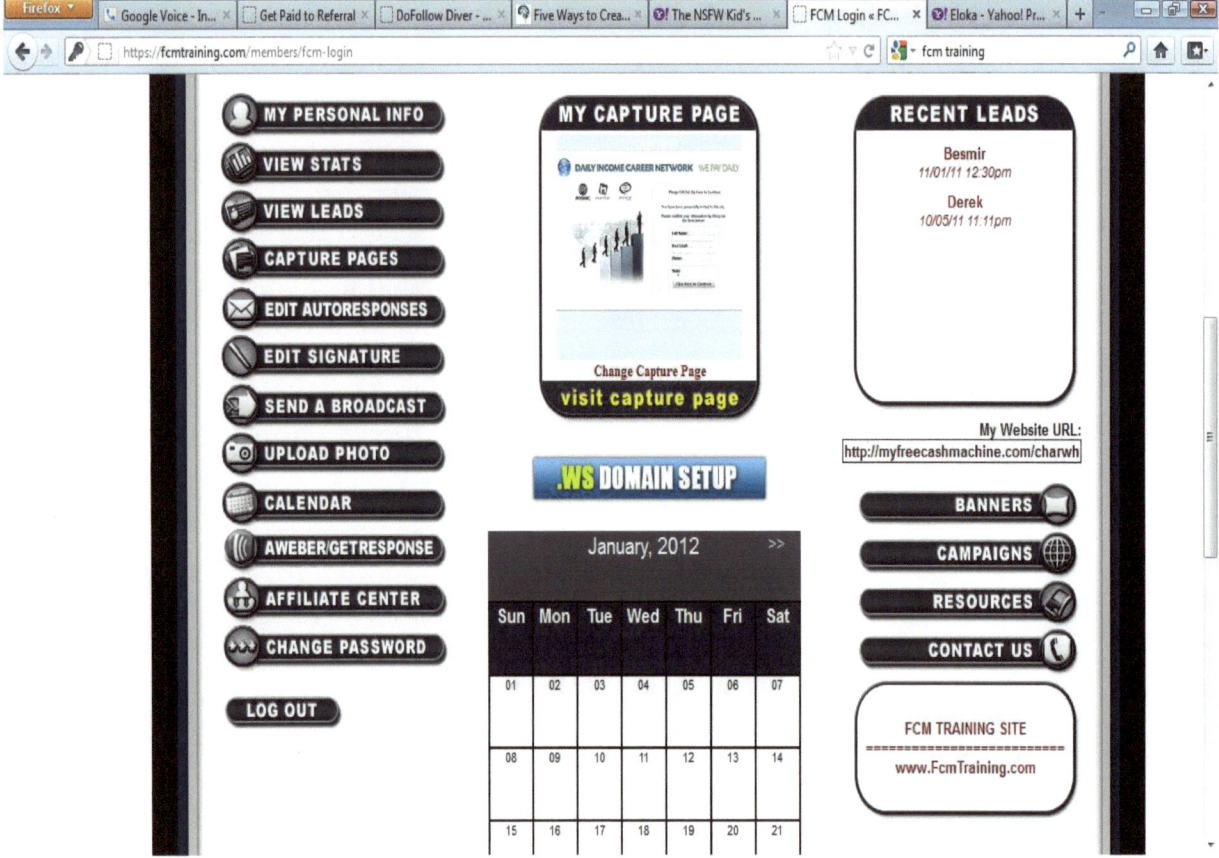

This is one of the companies I do for the long term. Some of them are free like the Netflix Trial, but the reward is $480. You can change your prize to a XBOX 360.

Visit: http://tinyurl.com/7knkdtg

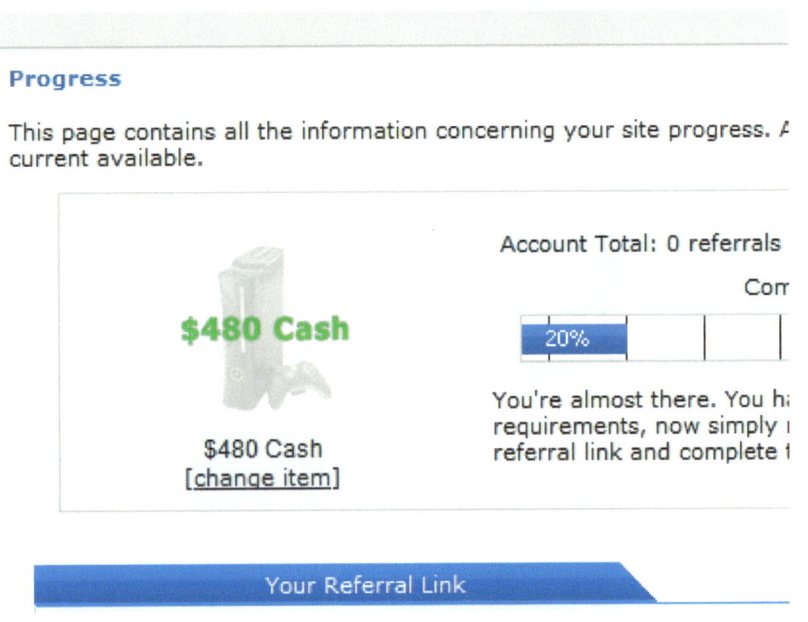

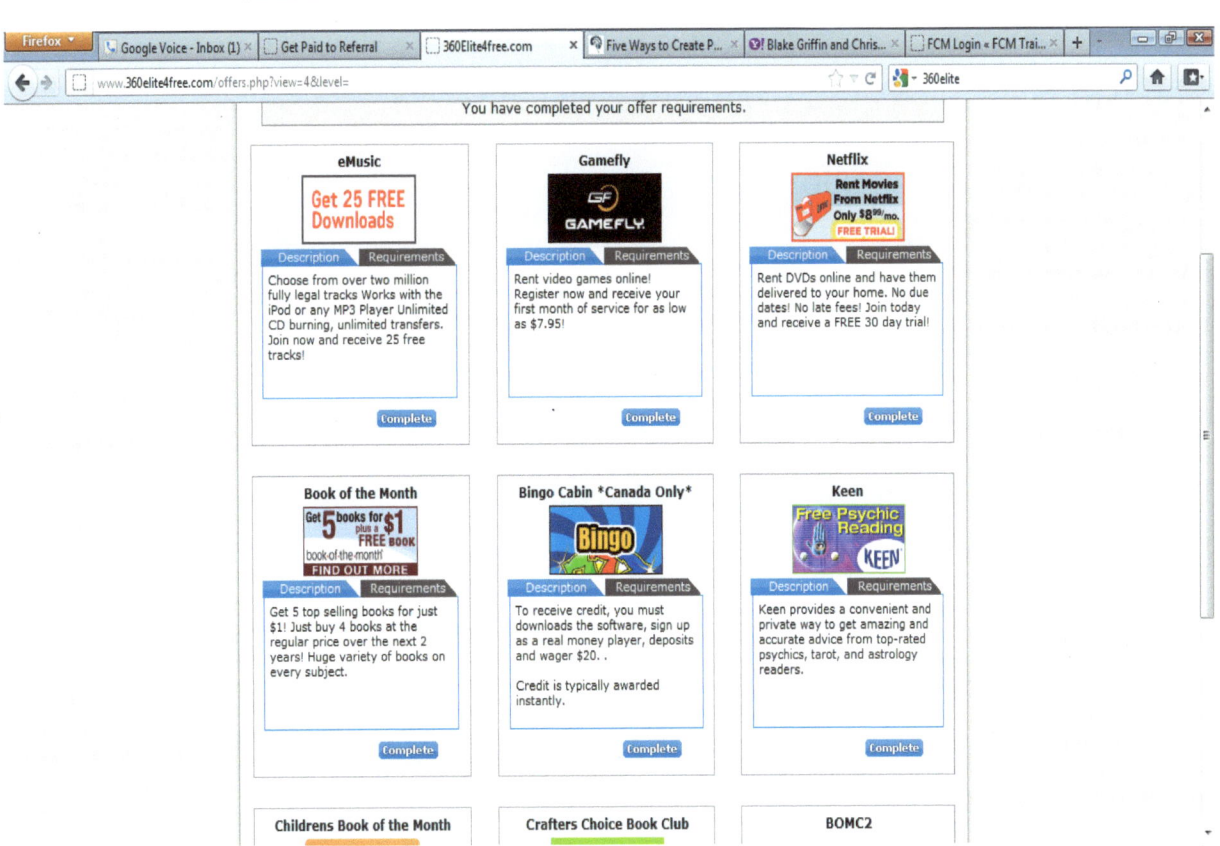

OPDS Advanced Marketing Training

This method involving craigslist may seem very simplistic, but these few minor "tweaks" can make the difference between you placing tons of free ads with online classified sites, making nothing, or making the type of income you saw on the video at: www.IncomeCrazy123.com

None of this information will violate the Terms and Conditions of either Craigslist. There are tons of e-books on how to "beat craigslist" and so on, but that is not what we are teaching here.

Using Craigslist to Get Referrals

You will need to create a Craigslist account.

Go to: www.craigslist.org

Posting ads in is the job section under Sales/Biz Development, Administrative and Customer Service sections generate the highest volume of responses. Even though this is NOT a job, we can still acquire a ton of prospects from this section who are very much looking for an opportunity like this, which literally is doing clerical work from home, on a computer.

With Craigslist, you can post ads for free if you post it in the smaller cities. Or, if you place your ad in a big city, it can cost around $25. The whole premise of this system, is that is all suppose to be free, but the advantage to actually paying for a Craigslist ad in a big city like LA, Chicago, New York, etc, is that you will get a TON of exposure to people who absolutely NEED an opportunity like this. So, what's $25, when that money is essentially made back four times over with 1 ZNZ One and 1 ZNZ Big Cash Sign up.

Here are a few tips that will save you a ton of time and frustration. Adhere to these tips to dramatically reduce the chances that your ads get flagged, or "ghosted".

WARNING: Do not post more than 5 ads. If you do, you risk getting your ads blocked.

WARNING: DO NOT POST YOUR REFERRAL OR WEBSITE LINK IN THE AD. You have been warned.

WARNING: DO NOT MENTION THE COMPANY NAME IN YOUR AD. Again, you have been warned.

WARNING: YOU MUST CHANGE THE TITLE OF THE AD EVERY TIME YOU POST IT OR IT WILL BE BLOCKED.

Step 1 – Post Your Ads

Here is the ad to post (Change the title to something a little different each time you post an ad, and do not post any website links):

Title: Customer Service Agents…$20/Hour

(or you can also use something like "internet based referral agent", or "referral agent", etc. Mix it up as you place more ads)

Body:

If you are dedicated, hard-working and ready to take on a new opportunity, this just might be the right fit for you!

You must be outgoing as well as possess a willingness to stick through until the end.

This is a work from home position, and there is no experience required.

Requirements:

Computer with internet connection
Knowledge of email usage
Basic Knowledge of the Internet

For more info please email us and one of our sponsors
will get back with you shortly

Step 2 – Set up your new Gmail account

Set up a Gmail account and add the message below as a vacation reply:

PLEASE NOTE: THIS WORK CANNOT BE PERFORMED FROM MOBILE INTERNET

Hello you replied to an ad on Craigslist about a position from home.

I will be your direct sponsor to help you get up and running, the same day you start.

You can contact me via email until we get you signed up.

This position does not require any out of pocket money what so ever.

What you will be doing is simply placing ads in classified sites like Craigslist, BackPage and other places as well exposing people to this free exciting opportunity.

We provide the ads needed to be posted!

You set your own hours but a minimum of 2 hours per day is required to succeed.

I have been with the team for about 6 months.

Average Pay Is $20 Per Hour or more!

In order to get started you will need these items and here are the reasons for them:

1. A PayPal Account: This is so you can be paid. But you can also have a check mailed. PayPal is a lot faster and usually same day.

If you don't have PayPal or AlertPay, don't worry this can be set up later

2. You can also choose AlertPay. That way your money goes direct deposit! www.alertpay.com

I will personally talk to you via email to be sure that the day you start work will be the day you get paid!

I personally walk you through the process. Takes about 20 Minutes to get going

Average person makes anywhere between $100-$300 a day

To let me know that you are serious about this opportunity I send you one step at a time. I do not want to waste my time with anyone.

If you wish to continue please reply to this email "Step One"

I look forward to working with you.

Your name

Your Email

===

Drastically Increase Conversions of your Craigslist Responses

You will quickly see that it is not difficult to get droves of responses from your craigslist ads. However, getting people to complete their ZNZ credits so you can be paid is a different story. Even though this is completely free, some people still need help, and extra support to get it done. To assist you with this, I created an email I send out to every new person that joins my team in ZNZ. I have included this email copy below with the header **"Welcome Email"**

Simply copy and paste the "welcome email" below into an actual email, that goes out to each new person who joins with you in ZNZ (send it back to them in real time as they sign up with you in ZNZ). You will notice the email comes with a list of all the current "free" offers (and the offers locations within the offer pages) a prospect can complete to get their credits (you will want to monitor and edit this list as offers in ZNZ always change). It also comes with a video tutorial that will show a person how to complete their offer credits in ZNZ Big Cash, which is the hardest one to complete, but pays us the most money. The video tutorial also shows them how to submit missing credit requests if they did an offer and did not receive a credit for it.

This simple email has helped me convert a ton of people from just regular sign ups, to those who complete their credits, which is how we GET PAID! The easier you can make it for people, the more likely they are to complete it. And the more people that complete their credits, the more money you will make.

Convert Even More Sign-Ups

Adding to the previous section, getting traffic and interested people is not hard to do with Craigslist. Getting those people to convert and complete offers can be the challenging part. As far as the offers go, your prospects are free to complete whatever offers they want, and we are not suppose to technically "recommend" or play favorites with any offers. (The list of offers in my "Welcome Email" simply point out the location and names of the free offers but doesn't technically recommend them).

Most of the time there is usually enough free offers in ZNZ One and Big Cash for your prospects to complete the necessary 1.00 offer credits in both, without having to pay anything at all. But, in my experience it is sometimes a lot easier and faster to have your prospects complete paid offers and just reimburse them out of your commission from ZNZ.

There are many discounted price trial offers that are around $1 to $5 each. You will earn around $100 to $104 per person who completes their credits in ZNZ one and Big Cash, so it is really no big deal to spend between $5 and $10 to earn 10X's that back in return. And the paid offers usually credit a lot faster than the free offers, which means you get paid quicker, and your new teammate is off and running quicker too!

So, just think about this; for every $1,000 you make, you would spend approximately $50 to $100 in reimbursing your teammates for paid offers they did. And this money isn't really coming out of your pocket ahead of time, it is coming out of the commission you make AFTER they complete the offers.

Note: You can only complete an offer one time. If your prospect attempts to complete the same offer on both ZNZ One and Big Cash, neither of you will receive credit.

This system is intended to help people. Don't be greedy. Don't try and start out doing thousands of dollars in one week when you've only been making a few hundred dollars per month. Start out slow then gradually increase.

If you have people that have been sitting on the fence offer to pay their way in using the method above. I would not suggest offering this to everyone that opt-in.

WELCOME EMAIL

SUBJECT LINE: Quick/Easy Offers For ZNZ Credit

BODY:

Hi,

Welcome to my ZNZ Team! If you haven't started doing so already, you'll want to complete your offer requirements so you can start making money too.

Completing the offers in ZNZ is actually very easy. I cannot technically recommend certain offers to you, but what will do is give you a list of the F.REE offers in ZNZ One and Big Cash, that will allow you to reach your credit requirements without spending any money.

*** OFFERS ARE CONSTANTLY BEING ADDED AND REMOVED, IF YOU END UP PAYING FOR AN OFFER(S) TO GET YOUR CREDIT REQUIREMENTS FULFILLED , LET ME KNOW AND I WILL PERSONALLY REIMBURSE YOU ***

For more detail about this, or if you get stuck doing your Big Cash offers, watch this video: http://www.byoaudio.com/playv/WM5h6Bss

For ZNZ One, you can usually only just do one offer as long as it's an offer that equals 1.0 credits. I personally did the creditreport.com offer because it is easy, free and is worth 1.0 credits (which will put you at your qualification requirements).

For ZNZ Big Cash, you still need to meet the total of 1.0 credits, but each offer is worth less, so you end up needing to do about 5-7 of the free offers to get to 1.00 credits total. Here's a list of the easiest free ones to reach your 1.00 credit requirements status.

Smart Credit (.25 credits) - Offer page 1

Equifax (.20 credits) - Offer page 1

Bill My Parents (.15 credits) - Offer page 1

Fun Pass (.15 credits) - Offer page 1

Time 4 Titles (.10 credits) - Offer page 1

Your Online Quote.com (.10 credits) - Offer page 1

Auto Quotes USA (.05 credits) - Offer Page 1

***Again, if you get stuck while doing your Big Cash offers, please watch this video: http://www.byoaudio.com/playv/WM5h6Bss ***

It's okay to do more than 1.00 credits, which is fine. It doesn't have to be 1.00 exactly. All of these offers are on the first page of your ZNZ Big Cash "offers" page within your ZNZ big cash back office. You will want to keep the welcome emails from all of your offers, so you can make sure to cancel them before their trial period expires (if you don't plan on keeping the product or service).

If you do any of the paid offers that are anywhere between $1 and $3, I will gladly reimburse you via PayPal or AlertPay. I keep money in both those accounts, just for that purpose.

You only need to do this offer process one time, and then you're set to make money without ever having to do this again. It's well worth the 25 minutes or so it will take you to complete all of them.

The marketing system will not do you any good until your qualifications are met within ZNZ one and ZNZ big cash. You are not in an earning position until you have reached 1.0 credits in each site.

Please let me know if you have any other questions.

Regards,

(Your Name)

Press Release Sites

	Directory	PR	Free	Comments
1	http://www.npr.org/	9	Yes	
2	http://www.betanews.com	6	Yes	
3	http://www.directionsmag.com	6	Yes	* Register
4	http://news.thomasnet.com/	6	Yes	
5	http://www.nanotech-now.com	6	Yes	
6	http://www.prlog.org/	6	Yes	* Register
7	http://www.downloadjunction.com	6	Yes	
8	http://www.newswiretoday.com/	6	Yes	* Register
9	http://www.pr-inside.com/	6	Yes	* Register
10	http://www.24-7pressrelease.com	6	Yes	* Register
11	http://www.pr.com/	6	Yes	* Register
12	http://www.prleap.com/	5	Yes	* Register
13	http://www.free-press-release.com/	5	Yes	* Register
14	http://www.clickpress.com/	5	Yes	* Register
15	http://www.pressbox.co.uk/	5	Yes	

16	http://www.filecluster.com/	5	Yes	
17	http://digitalmediaonlineinc.com/	5	Yes	* Register
18	http://www.onlineprnews.com/	5	Yes	* Register
19	http://www.i-newswire.com/	5	Yes	* Register
20	http://www.cgidir.com/	5	Yes	* Register
21	http://www.przoom.com/	5	Yes	* Register
22	http://www.openpr.com/	4	Yes	
23	http://www.sbwire.com/	4	Yes	* Register
24	http://www.1888pressrelease.com/	4	Yes	* Register
25	http://www.theopenpress.com/	4	Yes	* Register
26	http://www.free-press-release-center.info/	4	Yes	* Register
27	http://www.prfree.com/	4	Yes	* Register
28	http://www.ukprwire.com/	4	Yes	* Register
29	http://www.itbsoftware.com/	4	Yes	
30	http://www.itbinternet.com	4	Yes	
31	http://www.freepressreleases.co.uk/	4	Yes	* Register
32	http://freepressindex.com/	4	Yes	* Register

#	URL			
33	http://www.prwindow.com/	4	Yes	* Register
34	http://www.prurgent.com/	4	Yes	* Register
35	http://www.freepressrelease.com.au/	4	Yes	* Register
36	http://www.afreego.com/	3	Yes	
37	http://pressabout.com/	3	Yes	* Register
38	http://www.pressmethod.com/	3	Yes	* Register
39	http://pr-gb.com/	3	Yes	* Register
40	http://www.pressexposure.com/	3	Yes	
41	http://www.mediasyndicate.com	3	Yes	* Register
42	http://prmac.com/	3	Yes	* Register
43	http://www.publicitywires.com/	3	Yes	* Register
44	http://www.seenation.com/	3	Yes	* Register
45	http://www.afly.com/	3	Yes	* Register
46	http://www.addpr.com/	3	Yes	* Register
47	http://www.pressreleasecirculation.com/	3	Yes	
48	http://jkhanok.com/	3	Yes	
49	http://news.eboomwebsolutions.com/	2	Yes	* Register

50	http://emeapr.com/	1	Yes	* Register

Listed brought to you by: http://www.avangate.com/articles/press-release-distribution.htm